**BOLD KIDS**

# Airplanes

## A PLANES & AVIATION FACTS AND PICTURE BOOK FOR CHILDREN

Children are fascinated by the wonder of airplanes. They love to make paper airplanes to play with and learn about the fascinating world of airplanes. The world of flight is full of amazing facts, and you can teach your children about airplanes through fun activities.

These Facts About Planes for Kids can help them learn more about airplanes and aviation. Listed below are some of the most fascinating facts about airplanes.

The first motor-powered aircraft flew 120 feet in 12 seconds, making Orville Wright the first person to achieve flight. Wilbur Wright also tried flying his creation, but he failed. Although he did not succeed, the fact that it flew so high is still a fascinating accomplishment.

For kids, it is important to understand the importance of aviation. This is because airplanes use the power of gravity to overcome the forces of air resistance.

**A**irplanes are large flying machines, powered by engines and wing flaps. These machines propel through the air using the force of thrust from their engines. They are used for transportation, recreation, military use, research, and other purposes.

The Wright brothers were the first to fly an airplane. They were the first to successfully fly a plane and the world changed forever. And today, millions of people use airplanes for travel, recreation, and research.

**A**irplanes are a type of flying machine that generates thrust through the air by the use of propellers, wings, and air support. The first manned flight occurred in the 18th century by hot-air balloon.

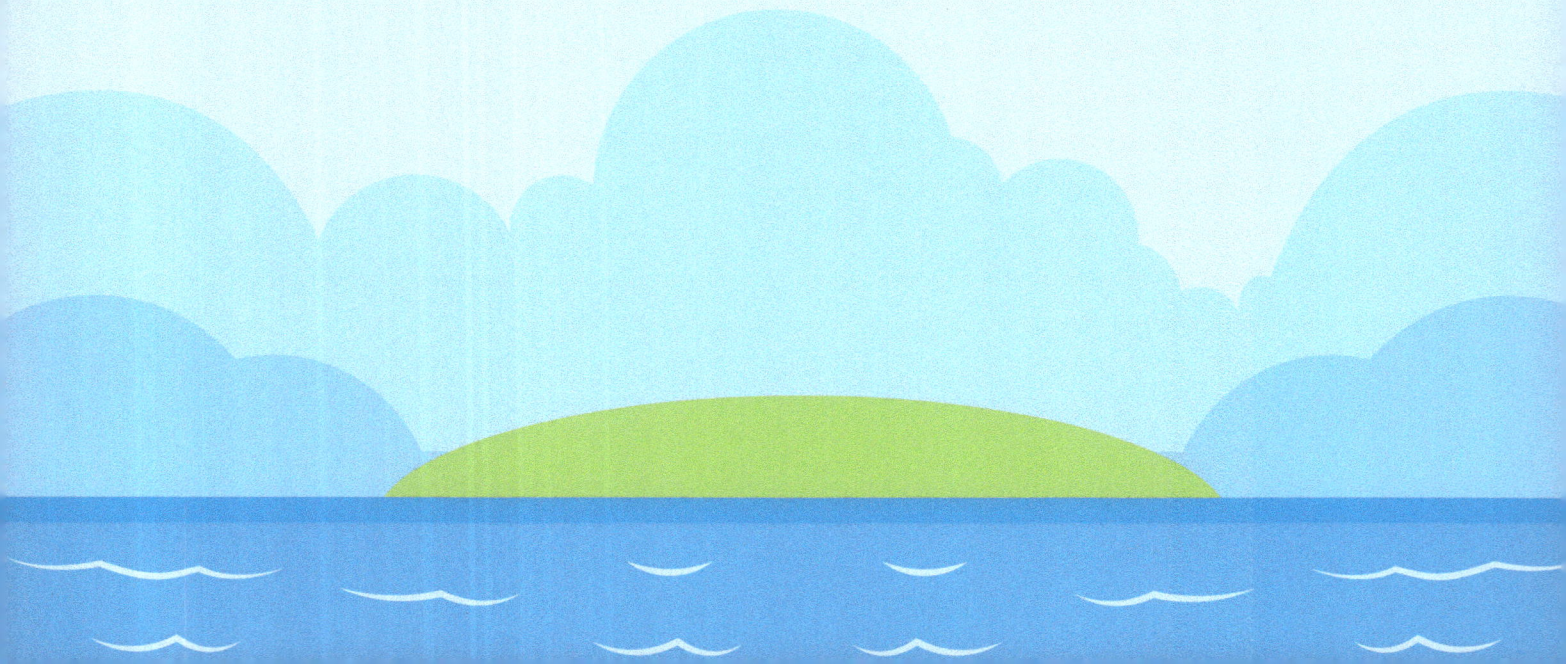

There were various types of airplanes used for research and transportation. The Wright Flyer was the first one to fly for 12 seconds and 120 feet. Throughout history, planes have been used for research, recreation, and military purposes.

An airplane is a fixed-wing flying vehicle that uses an engine to provide thrust in the air. Its wings create lift and help the aircraft overcome drag. It is also one of the most common types of flying vehicles.

Its fixed wings allow the airplane to maneuver from one place to another. While there are many types of airplanes, they are the most commonly used type of aircraft. The Wright Brothers invented the first airplane in 1903.

The Wright brothers were inspired to build an airplane by reading a book on aerodynamics by Otto Lienthal. They used the book to inspire the Wright Brothers. In addition to being a great way to learn about the history of airplanes, it also helps your child learn about the importance of airplanes to the world.

Its unique design makes it a popular choice among many children. If you want to know more about the origins of planes, check out these Facts About Aerial Vehicles for Kids

**A** plane uses fixed wings and engines to propel itself through the air. Like birds, airplanes have many uses. These aircraft are used for transportation, recreation, and research.

While most aircraft are used for commercial purposes, the Wright Flyer is the first airplane to fly. It flew for 12 seconds and a distance of 120 feet. The first commercial aircraft was built in 1926. The invention of the airplane allowed it to fly in the sky.

An airplane is a fixed-winged flying vehicle that uses a series of engines to produce thrust in the air. Its wings provide lift, which allows it to fly from one point to another. A plane is an amazing machine and it does many things!

**B**ut the flight you make with it is the best part. With an airplane, you'll never be bored again. In fact, it's a wonderful way to teach your kids about the world of aviation.

Kids love airplanes and their amazing wings! The fact about airplanes that you teach them will make learning about airplanes more fun. If you're interested in learning about the history of aviation, there are lots of fun and educational facts about airplanes.

For example, they can learn about the different types of commercial aircraft and drones. And, they can learn about the different parts of an airplane.

Lightning Source UK Ltd.
Milton Keynes UK
UKHW050838210223
417371UK00008B/119

9 781071 708637